101 Fruit Recipes

by Carole Eberly

Cover by Kathi Terry

Illustrations by Gerry Wykes

Copyright 1983, 1994 by **eberly press**

1004 Michigan Ave.

East Lansing, MI 48823

ISBN-0-932296-09-2

TABLE OF CONTENTS

Best time to buy fruit 3
Fresh fruit availability 4
Apples 5
Apricots 15
Blueberries 19
Cantaloupe 27
Cherries 33
Cranberries 39
Grapes 47
Peaches 51
Pears 59
Plums 65
Raspberries 69
Rhubarb 75
Strawberries 81
Watermelon 93

BEST TIMES TO BUY FRESH FRUIT

Listed below are the best times to buy fresh fruit—meaning this time period is when most of the fruit is ripened. The fresh fruit availability list means these fruits are available in supermarkets and farm markets because they're shipped or are special varieties.

Apples	August-October
Apricots	July-August
Blueberries	July-August
Cantaloupe	August-September
Cherries (Sweet)	June-July
Cherries (Tart)	June-July
Cranberries	October-January
Grapes (Concord)	September-October
Grapes (Thompson-Seedless)	June-November
Peaches	July-September
Pears	August-September
Plums	August-September
Raspberries	July
Rhubarb	May-June
Strawberries	May-June
Watermelon	August-October

FRESH FRUIT AVAILABILITY

Apples	August-April
Apricots	May-September
Blueberries	June-August
Cantaloupe	May-December
Cherries (Sweet)	May-August
Cherries (Tart)	June-August
Cranberries	September-February
Grapes (Concord)	September-October
Grapes (Thompson-Seedless)	June-November
Peaches	May-October
Pears	July-May
Plums	June-October
Raspberries	May-September
Rhubarb	May-August
Strawberries	May-December
Watermelon	July-November

Apples

HOT SPICED CIDER

1 gallon apple cider
1 c. brown sugar
2 sticks cinnamon
10 whole cloves

Bring cider to a boil. Add remaining ingredients and simmer over low heat, stirring until sugar dissolves. Strain. Serves 16.

SWEDISH APPLE PIE

(This is a great recipe for bakers who turn out less than perfect pie crusts.)

8 apples, pared, cored & sliced
1 T sugar
1 t cinnamon
1/2 c. soft butter
1 c. sugar
1/4 t salt
1 egg
1 c. flour
1/2 c. chopped walnuts

Put sliced apples in buttered 10-inch pie plate. Mix sugar and cinnamon, sprinkle over apples. Cream butter, 1 c. sugar, salt and egg. Mix in flour. Spread over apples. Sprinkle walnuts over top. Bake at 350 degrees for 45-50 minutes.

APPLE GOODIE

6 c. sliced, pared apples
1 1/2 c. sugar
1 1/2 t cinnamon
2 T flour
1 c. oatmeal

3/4 c. brown sugar
3/4 c. flour
1/4 t baking powder
1/2 t baking soda
1/2 c. soft butter

Mix together first four ingredients and place in buttered casserole dish. Mix remaining ingredients together until crumbly. Sprinkle on top of apple mixture and pat down. Bake one hour at 350 degrees. Serve hot or cold with whipped cream or ice cream.

GOOEY APPLE DESSERT
(Guaranteed to add at least one inch to your hips!)

1 1/2 c. brown sugar
1 T cornstarch
1/2 t salt
2 c. cold water
1 t vanilla
2 T butter
2 c. flour
1/4 c. sugar

1 T baking powder
1/3 c. soft butter
3 c. chopped, peeled apples
3/4 c. milk
1/2 t vanilla
1 T sugar
1/2 t cinnamon
2 T butter

In a saucepan, mix together brown sugar, cornstarch, salt and water. Cook until boiling. Cook an additional two minutes, stirring constantly. Mix in teaspoon vanilla and two tablespoons butter. Pour into a 9x13" baking dish. In a bowl, mix together flour, sugar, baking powder and butter. Stir in apples, milk and vanilla until moistened. Drop by tablespoons over syrup. Combine sugar and cinnamon. Sprinkle on top. Dot with butter and bake for 50 minutes at 350 degrees. Serves 10.

GERMAN APPLE PANCAKE

2 eggs
1/2 c. flour
1/2 c. milk
1/4 t salt
1 T butter
1 c. brown sugar

2 T cornstarch
1/2 t cinnamon
1/2 c. milk
1/4 c. butter
4 c. sliced, peeled apples

Beat eggs, flour, milk and salt until smooth. Melt 1 T. butter in oven proof skillet and coat well. Pour in batter and bake at 450 degrees for 10 minutes. Reduce heat to 350 degrees and bake 10 more minutes, or until golden brown. Meanwhile, mix sugar, cornstarch and cinnamon. Blend in milk and butter; cook over medium heat until thickened. Add apples and simmer until apples are tender. Spoon half of the sauce over pancake. Cut into wedges and serve with remaining sauce. Serves 6.

APPLE FRITTERS

1 c. cottage cheese
2 eggs
1 c. grated, peeled apples
1/4 t salt
1/4 t cinnamon
1/4 t nutmeg
1 t sugar
1 c. flour
1 t baking soda
Powdered sugar
Sour cream

Beat together cottage cheese, eggs and apples. Sift dry ingredients together, except powdered sugar. Add to apple mixture alternately with 1/4 c. sour cream. Drop by tablespoon into oil heated to 375 degrees. Brown, turn and drain on paper towels. Sift powdered sugar over fritters and serve with extra sour cream, if desired. Makes 4-6 servings.

APPLESAUCE BUTTERSCOTCH CHIP CAKE

1/2 c. butter
1 c. sugar
2 eggs
1 3/4 c. flour
1 t baking soda
1 t cinnamon
1/4 t salt
1/4 t ground cloves
1 c. applesauce
1/2 c. raisins
1/2 c. chopped walnuts
1 6-oz. pkg. butterscotch chips

Cream butter and sugar. Add eggs, beating well. Sift together dry ingredients. Add alternately with applesauce to butter mixture. Stir in raisins, walnuts and half of the butterscotch chips. Pour into a 9x5" greased loaf pan. Sprinkle remaining chips over top. Bake at 325 degrees about 1 hour and 15 minutes, or until done.

APPLESAUCE CHRISTMAS CAKE

(This is one of the weirder cakes I've made, but it's so easy, delicious...and rich—one small slice is all anyone needs. Of course, wants and needs are two different things.)

- 1 3-oz. pkg. lime gelatin
- 1 3-oz. pkg. raspberry gelatin
- 1 15-oz. jar applesauce
- 18 double graham crackers
- 1 c. whipped cream
- 3 T powdered sugar
- 1/4 t almond extract

Place lime and raspberry gelatin in separate bowls. Add 3/4 c. applesauce to each and mix thoroughly. Place two double crackers end to end on serving dish. Spread with 1/4 c. lime gelatin mixture. Top with layer of crackers and repeat with 1/4 c. raspberry gelatin. Repeat layers, ending with crackers. Whip cream, adding powdered sugar and almond extract before spreading over top and sides of loaf. Chill one hour. Serves 12-14.

CIDER APPLE SALAD

2 1/2 c. cider
2 T unflavored gelatin
1/4 t salt
1 c. diced apples
1/4 c. chopped walnuts
1/2 c. diced celery

Dissolve gelatin in 1/2 c. cold cider. Add 2 c. boiling cider and stir well. Add salt. Chill until slightly thickened, stirring occasionally. Add remaining ingredients and refrigerate until set.

APPLE POTATO SALAD

3/4 c. mayonnaise
3/4 c. sour cream
4 oz. blue cheese, crumbled
1 t salt
1/2 t dillweed
2 apples, chopped
2 T lemon juice
6 c. cubed, cooked potatoes
3 c. cooked, cubed ham

Mix together mayonnaise, sour cream, blue cheese, salt and dillweed. Sprinkle lemon juice over apples. Add to dressing with potatoes and ham. Chill. Serves 6.

APPLE AND HAM PIE

Pastry for 2-crust pie
3 c. apples, peeled and sliced
2/3 c. brown sugar
1 T flour
1 t cinnamon
1/4 t nutmeg
1 c. diced, cooked ham

Line pie plate with crust. Sprinkle with a little sugar. Spread with half the apples and cover with half the sugar, flour and spices. Add ham. Repeat with another layer of apples, sugar, flour and spices. Cover with top crust and cut in steam vents. Bake at 425 degrees for 15 minutes. Lower heat to 350 degrees and bake 30-45 more minutes.

APPLE CAKE

(This cake requires no icing because the cake has its own crunchy topping.)

1 c. sugar
1/4 c. butter
1 egg
1 c. flour
1 t baking soda
1/2 t cinnamon
5 peeled and chopped apples
1 c. chopped walnuts

Cream butter and sugar. Add egg and beat well. Sift dry ingredients together and mix in with a spoon. Stir in apples and walnuts. Bake in buttered casserole dish at 350 degrees for 25-30 minutes.

Apricots

APRICOT TARTS

2 t unflavored gelatin
3 T sugar
1 1/4 c. orange juice
1/4 t nutmeg
1 1/2 c. pitted, sliced apricots
6 tart shells, baked

Combine gelatin, sugar and 1/4 c. orange juice in saucepan over low heat until gelatin is dissolved. Remove from heat and stir in remaining orange juice and nutmeg. Chill until slightly thickened. Place tarts on cookie sheet and fill with fruit. Spoon orange glaze over fruit. Chill until set.

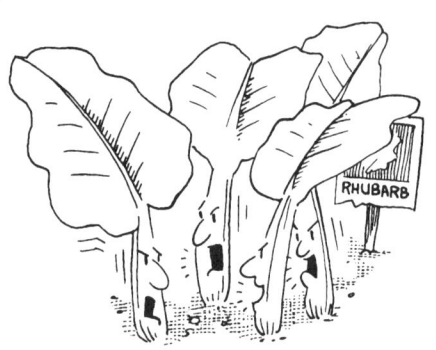

APRICOT BREAD

1 c. dried apricots
1 c. sugar
2 T soft butter
1 egg
3/4 c. orange juice
2 c. flour
2 t baking powder
1/4 t baking soda
1 t salt
1/2 c . chopped walnuts

Soak apricots until soft. Cut into small pieces. Beat together sugar, butter, egg and orange juice. Sift dry ingredients and combine with other mixture. Stir in walnuts. Pour into buttered loaf pan. Bake for one hour at 350 degrees.

APRICOT PIE

Pastry for 2-crust pie
2 1/2 c. fresh apricots
1 1/2 T cornstarch
1/2 t cinnamon
1/2 t nutmeg
1/4 t salt
3/4 c. sugar
Butter

Pit fruit and cut in halves. Mix with remaining ingredients. Pour fruit mixture into pie pan and dot with butter. Put on top crust, making vents for steam. Bake at 400 degrees for 40-45 minutes.

APRICOT BROWN BETTY

2 c. dried apricots
2 c. dry bread crumbs
1/4 c. melted butter
1/2 c. brown sugar
1 t cinnamon
1/2 c. hot water from apricots
Juice from 1/2 lemon

Soak apricots in hot water. Mix crumbs and butter; cover bottom of baking dish with 1/2 of mixture. Drain apricots, reserving 1/2 c. liquid. Spread half the apricots over crumbs. Sprinkle with half the sugar, cinnamon, apricot liquid and lemon juice. Repeat and top with remaining bread crumbs. Bake 20 minutes at 350 degrees covered. Uncover and bake for 20 more minutes.

Blueberries

BLUEBERRY PIE

Pastry for 2-crust pie
4 c. blueberries
3/4 c. sugar
3 T flour
1/2 t cinnamon
1/2 t nutmeg
Dash salt
2 t lemon juice
1 T butter

Mix together blueberries, sugar, flour, cinnamon, nutmeg and salt. Pour into pie shell. Sprinkle with lemon juice and dot with butter. Place top crust on. Bake at 400 degrees 35 minutes.

BLUEBERRY MUFFINS

2 1/2 c. flour
2 1/2 t baking powder
1/4 t salt
3/4 c. sugar, divided
1 c. buttermilk
2 eggs, beaten
1/2 c. salad oil
1 1/2 c. blueberries

Sift together flour, baking powder, salt and 1/2 c. sugar. Add buttermilk, eggs and oil, mixing only until dry ingredients are damp. Gently fold in berries. Spoon into greased muffin tins, filling 2/3 full. Sprinkle with remaining sugar. Bake at 400 degrees for 20-25 minutes. Makes about 16.

COLD BLUEBERRY SOUP

2 c. blueberries
1 1/2 c. water
1/3 c. sugar
1/4 t lemon juice
1 cinnamon stick
3/4 c. sour cream

Combine all ingredients, except sour cream, in a saucepan. Bring to a boil and simmer 15 minutes. Remove cinnamon stick and pour into blender. Blend. Chill 3-4 hours. Just before serving, stir in sour cream. Makes about 3 1/2 cups.

BLUEBERRY PANCAKES

1 1/4 c. flour
3 t baking powder
1 T sugar
1/2 t salt
1 egg, beaten
1 c. milk
2 T salad oil
1 c. blueberries

Sift dry ingredients together. Combine egg, milk and salad oil; add to dry ingredients, stirring just until flour is damp. Gently fold in blueberries. Bake on hot griddle. Makes about 8-10 pancakes. Serve with blueberry syrup for a real treat.

BLUEBERRY SYRUP

2 c. blueberries
1 c. water
3/4 c. sugar
1/2 t lemon juice

Place all ingredients in a saucepan and cook over low heat until sauce is syrupy—about 20-30 minutes. Stir to keep from sticking. *Great on pancakes, waffles or ice cream.*

BLUEBERRY SALAD

1 c. sour cream	1/4 t cinnamon
2 T corn syrup	2 c. blueberries
1 t lemon juice	2 c. diced cantaloupe
1/4 t nutmeg	2 c. green grapes

In a small bowl, combine sour cream, corn syrup, lemon juice and spices. In a medium bowl, mix fruit together. Pour sour cream sauce over fruit and mix well. Makes 6 cups.

BLUEBERRY PEACH JAM

3 c. blueberries
2 c. peaches, pitted and peeled
1 pkg. fruit pectin
1/4 t cinnamon
7 c. sugar

Crush blueberries in a medium saucepan. Cut peaches into pieces and grind in food mill. Add to blueberries. Mix fruit pectin and cinnamon with fruit and cook over high heat until mixture comes to a boil, stirring constantly. Add sugar all at once. Bring to a full, rolling boil and boil hard one minute, stirring constantly. Remove from heat. Skim and stir to remove foam. Ladle into hot jars. Makes 8 8-oz. jars.

BLUEBERRY COFFEECAKE

1 c. flour
1 1/4 t baking powder
1/4 t salt
1/4 c. soft butter
1/2 c. sugar
1 egg
1 t grated lemon peel
1/4 t nutmeg
1/4 c. milk
1/2 t lemon extract
3/4 c. blueberries
1 T sugar

Sift together flour, baking powder and salt. Set aside. Beat butter and sugar until creamy. Add in egg, lemon peel and nutmeg. Beat until well blended. Stir in the flour mixture, milk and extract. Fold in blueberries. Spread batter in a buttered 8-inch cake pan. Sprinkle with 1 T sugar and bake at 350 degrees for 30-35 minutes.

BLUEBERRY GRUNT

3 c. blueberries
4 t lemon juice
1/2 c. sugar
1/4 t cinnamon
1/4 t nutmeg
1 c. flour
2 T sugar
1 1/2 t baking powder
Dash salt
1/4 c. soft butter
1/2 c. milk
1 beaten egg

Mix together blueberries, lemon juice, sugar and spices. Pour into a buttered casserole dish. In a medium bowl combine flour, sugar, baking powder and salt. Mix in butter. Add remaining ingredients and stir until just moistened. Spread over the berries and bake at 425 for 20 minutes. Serves 6.

Cantaloupe

SEMI-SCIENTIFIC MELON SELECTING

It's fairly easy to pick up a decent peach or pear at the market without much know-how. It simply looks right, feels ripe when you gently squeeze it and smells delicious.

But what about those darned melons—cantaloupes and watermelons? How in the world do you know what's inside the things. Will it be underripe and tasteless—not to mention so hard it could bend a spoon—or will it be overripe and squishy? Or, wonder of wonders, will it be just right?

Wonder no more. Those women you thought were nuts standing around sniffing cantaloupes and thumping watermelons were on the right track. Now you can be, too.

With cantaloupes, look for a distinctive raised, grayish netting pattern that stands out from a yellow-green—not dark green—background. As the melon ripens, the background will change to a more yellow color. When fully ripe, the blossom end will be slightly soft.

Now for the smell test. A ripe melon will have a heavy, sweet aroma—strongest at the stem end. Stay away from melons with any attached or withered stems showing. These were not mature when picked and will not ripen properly.

Whn eying watermelons, look for a heavy one, indicating juiciness. Pick one that has a yellow underside rather than a white one. When no one's looking, scratch the rind gently with your fingernail. If the peel comes off easily, the watermelon should be ripe.

Move right on past melons with spots of fungus on the rind—a sure sign they were stored too long at room temperature.

Now jump right in with the other smellers and thumpers.

SPICED CANTALOUPE

3 lbs. cantaloupe
2 t alum
2 qt. water
3 c. sugar
1 pt. cider vinegar
3 sticks cinnamon
1 T whole cloves
1 t allspice

Cut peeled cantaloupe into small squares. Bring alum and water to a boil. Add cantaloupe and cook 15 minutes. Drain well. Combine remaining ingredients. Add cantaloupe and cook over low heat until fruit is transparent, about 35 minutes. Ladle into hot, sterile jars and seal. Makes about 4 pints.

CANTALOUPE SAUCE

1 cantaloupe, peeled & cut into small cubes
Lemon juice
Sugar

Puree cantaloupe in blender. Add lemon juice and sugar to taste. Chill. A nice ice cream topping.

COLD MELON SOUP

1 cantaloupe
2 T lemon jucie
1 t chopped mint
1/8 t cinnamon
1/3 c. vanilla yogurt
1/3 c. cream

Peel and slice cantaloupe. Puree in blender with lemon juice, mint and cinnamon. Chill. Stir in yogurt and cream. Serves 4.

MELON PIE

9-inch baked pie shell
1 3-oz. pkg. lemon gelatin
1/2 c. heavy cream, whipped
1 c. cubed cantaloupe, well drained
1 c. cubed watermelon, well drained
1 c. cubed honeydew, well drained
1/4 t nutmeg

Prepare gelatin according to package directions, using only 1 1/2 c. water. Chill until slightly thickened. Fold in whipped cream and melons. Turn into baked pie shell. Chill several hours or until firm. Sprinkle with nutmeg.

Cherries

EASY CHERRY CAKE

1/2 c. butter
1 egg
1/2 c. milk
1 t almond extract
1 1/2 c. flour
1 t baking soda
1/4 t salt
1 c. tart cherries, pitted

Beat all ingredients together, except cherries. Pour into a greased cake pan. Top with cherries. Bake at 350 degrees for 25 minutes. Serve with whipped cream or cherry sauce.

CHERRY SAUCE

1/2 c. sugar
1 T cornstarch
1/2 c. water
2 c. tart cherries, pitted
1 T butter
1 T lemon juice

Cook sugar, cornstarch and water over low heat for 15 minutes, stirring constantly. Add remaining ingredients and cook until thick and hot. Makes about 3 cups.

OLD FASHIONED CHERRY PIE

Pastry & lattice top for 9-inch pie
3 c. tart cherries, pitted
1 c. sugar
1/2 c. flour
4 drops almond extract
1/8 t salt
1 1/2 T butter

Mix cherries together with sugar, flour, extract and salt. Pour into pastry shell. Dot with butter. Place lattice top on, sealing with water and crimping edges high. Bake at 425 degrees for 10 minutes. Reduce heat to 350 degrees and bake 30 minutes longer.

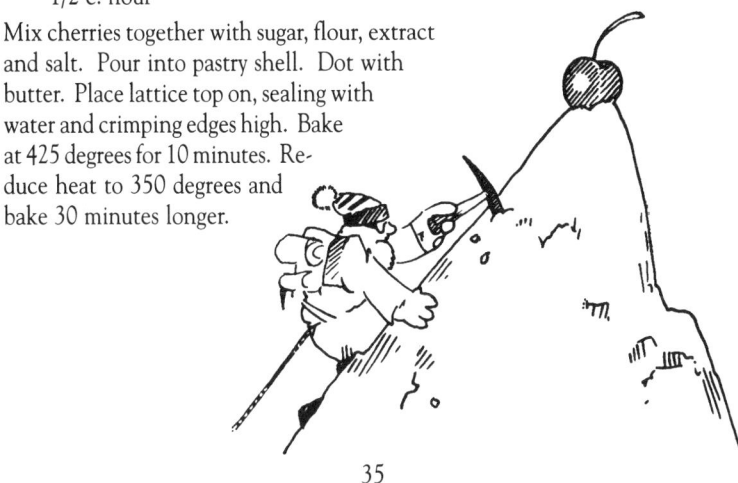

BLACK CHERRY BURGUNDY PIE

1 c. water
1/2 c. sugar
1 3-oz. pkg. cherry gelatin
2 c. sweet cherries, pitted
1 pt. vanilla ice cream
3 T burgundy
1 t lemon juice
1 9-inch baked pie shell

Boil water. Dissolve sugar and gelatin into it. Stir in cherries. Add ice cream by spoonfuls, stirring until melted. Blend in wine and lemon juice. Pour into pie shell and chill until set.

(Interesting item! Cherry pits were found among cave dweller's remains in Europe, North America and Asia.)

BRANDIED CHERRIES

5 c. sweet cherries
2 1/2 c. water
2 c. sugar
1/2 c. brandy

Pit cherries. Cook pits in water 15 minutes. Measure out 2 cups liquid and pour in saucepan. Add sugar. Boil 5 minutes, stirring occasionally. Add cherries and cook 10 minutes. Remove cherries. Cook syrup until thick. Pour over cherries. Mix in brandy. Serve over ice cream, pudding or pound cake. Makes 2 pints.

CHERRY BOUNCE
(Wonderful at Christmastime. Also makes a nice gift.)

2 qt. tart cherries
1 lb. sugar
2 fifths whiskey

Mix all ingredients together in a large glass jar or crock. Cover. Stir once a day for the first week. Stir once a week thereafter. Strain and bottle anytime after 2 months. Makes about 2 quarts.

CHERRY JUBILEE

1/2 c. sugar	1 lb. sweet cherries, pitted
1 T cornstarch	1/4 c. brandy
1 c. water	Ice cream

Cook sugar, cornstarch, water and cherries over medium heat until thickened, stirring constantly. Pour brandy over top. Ignite and spoon immediately over ice cream in individual serving dishes. Serves 4.

CHERRY-CHEESE SQUARES

1/2 c. soft butter	1 3-oz. pkg. cream cheese
1 1/2 c. flour	1 lb. tart cherries, pitted
2 T sugar	3 T cornstarch
1 3-oz. pkg. vanilla pudding	1 c. sugar
1 3/4 c. milk	1 T lemon juice

Mix butter, flour and sugar to make a dough. Pat in bottom of square baking dish. Bake at 350 degrees for 10 minutes. Cool. Combine pudding mix and milk in saucepan, cooking until thick. Beat in cream cheese, blending until smooth. Cool and pour over dough. Cool in refrigerator. Mix cherries with cornstarch, sugar and lemon juice in saucepan. Cook until thick and clear. Cool. Spread over top of pudding. Serves 8.

Cranberries

CRANBERRY BARS

1 c. oatmeal	1/3 c. butter
3/4 c. brown sugar	1/2 c. chopped walnuts
1/2 c. flour	1 c. whole cranberry sauce
1/2 c. coconut	1 T lemon juice

Mix oatmeal, sugar, flour, coconut and butter together until crumbly. Pat half the mixture in bottom of 9-inch baking pan. Mix walnuts, cranberry sauce and lemon juice together; spread on mixture in pan. Cover with remaining crumb mixture. Bake at 350 degrees for 35 minutes. Cut into bars and serve with whipped cream.

CRANBERRY NUT SALAD

1 qt. cranberries, raw	1 lb. green seedless grapes, halved
1 1/2 c. sugar	
1 lb. miniature marshmallows	1 pt. whipping cream, whipped
1 c. chopped walnuts	

Grind cranberries. Mix with sugar and let set 3-4 hours. Drain off juice and mix with remaining ingredients. Serve chilled. Serves 6-8.

CRANBERRY UPSIDE-DOWN CAKE

3 T. butter, melted
1 1/2 c. brown sugar
2 c. cranberries
1 1/2 c. flour
1 1/2 t baking powder
1/4 t salt
1/2 c. butter
1 egg
1/2 c. milk
1 t vanilla

Mix butter and 1 c. sugar together. Pour into bottom of baking pan. Sprinkle cranberries on top. Sift flour, baking powder and salt. Cream butter with 1/2 c. sugar and egg. Add dry ingredients alternately with milk and beat well. Add vanilla. Pour batter over cranberries and bake at 350 degrees 40-50 minutes. Turn upside down on serving platter. Serve with whipped cream.

CRANBERRY NUT LOAF

3 c. flour
1 c. sugar
1 t salt
1 T baking powder
1 t baking soda
1/2 c. shortening

1 1/4 c. milk
2 eggs
1 T grated orange rind
1/2 t cinnamon
1 c. cranberries
1/2 c. walnuts, chopped

Sift together flour, sugar, salt, baking powder and baking soda. Cut in shortening. Mix milk, eggs, orange rind and cinnamon together. Pour into dry mixture, stirring until just moistened. Fold in cranberries and nuts. Pour into buttered loaf pan. Bake at 350 degrees for 1 hour.

SPICED CRANBERRIES

2 1/2 qts. cranberries
5 c. sugar
2 t cinnamon
1/2 t cloves
1/4 t nutmeg
1 c. vinegar

Cook berries until soft. Stir in remaining ingredients, cooking almost to the jellying point and stirring frequently. Pour into hot, sterile jars. Makes about 7 8-oz. jars.

CRANBERRY RELISH

1 lb. cranberries
2 c. sugar
1 orange, unpeeled
2 apples, cored, unpeeled

Grind cranberries and mix with sugar. Finely chop orange and apples; mix with cranberries. Chill overnight. Makes about 4 cups.

CRANBERRY PUNCH

4 c. cranberry juice
2 6-oz. cans limeade
6 cans water
Orange slices
Cherries

Mix limeade, water and cranberry juice together. Pour into punch bowl and garnish with orange slices and cherries. Makes about 2 1/2 quarts.

CRANBERRY PIE

Pastry for 2-crust 9-inch pie
1 1/2 c. cranberries
1 c. raisins
1 c. water
1 c. sugar
3 T flour
2 T butter
2 t vanilla
1 t grated orange rind
1/4 t cinnamon
1 c. chopped walnuts

Boil together cranberries and raisins in 1 c. water until skins pop. Mix sugar and flour; add to cranberry mixture and cook a few minutes until slightly thickened. Remove from heat and stir in butter, vanilla, orange rind, cinnamon and walnuts. Pour into pie shell. Adjust top crust. Bake at 400 degrees 15 minutes; continue baking at 350 degrees 20-30 minutes more.

CRANBERRY APPLE PIE

Pastry for 2-crust, 9-inch pie
1 lb. whole cranberry sauce
3 apples, chopped
1/2 c. chopped walnuts
1/2 c. sugar
3 T flour
1 t cinnamon
2 T melted butter

Mix all ingredients together and pour into pie shell. Adjust top crust and bake at 425 degrees 45-50 minutes.

Grapes

CONCORD GRAPE PIE

Pastry & lattice top for 9-inch pie
3 c. Concord grapes
3/4 c. sugar
1 T flour
1 t grated lemon rind
1 t vanilla
1 egg, well beaten

Remove skin from grapes. Place pulp in saucepan and cook until seeds are free. Rub pulp through sieve to remove seeds. Cool. Add grape skins, sugar, flour, lemon rind, vanilla and egg to pulp, mixing well. Pour into pastry shell. Place lattice pastry on top and seal. Bake at 425 degrees for 50-60 minutes.

FROSTED GREEN GRAPES

Beat 1 egg white until fluffy. Dip small clusters of grapes into it and roll gently in sugar, coating evenly. Chill until dry. Use as garnish on salads or desserts.

GRAPE CREAM

2 c. green grapes
1/2 c. sour cream
3 T brown sugar
1/4 t ginger

Place grapes in serving bowl. Dab on cream. Mix brown sugar and ginger together. Sprinkle over cream. Serves 4.

GREEN GRAPE MIXTURE

    4 c. green grapes
    1 c. water
    4 c. sugar
    Juice of 1 lemon

Simmer grapes in water until tender. Add sugar and boil to the jellying point, about 220 degrees. Add lemon juice and boil for 5 minutes longer. Ladle into hot, sterile jars. Makes about 4-6 half-pints.

Peaches

PEACH PUDDING

2 T butter
6 slices bread
3 T sugar
1/2 t cinnamon
4 eggs, separated
2 c. milk
1 c. sugar
1 t vanilla
3 c. sliced apples

Butter bread; sprinkle with 3 T sugar and cinnamon. Cut into cubes. Place in bottom of buttered baking dish. Mix together egg yolks, milk, 1/2 c. sugar and vanilla. Pour over bread. Put baking dish inside a larger one filled with hot water. Bake at 350 degrees for 35 minutes. Beat egg whites until foamy; gradually beat in remaining sugar until whites hold stiff peaks. Arrange peach slices on mixture pulled from oven. Spread egg whites over the top. Return to oven and bake 15-20 minutes longer.

PEACH SAUCE

2 T butter
3 T brown sugar
1 T lemon juice
3 peaches, chopped
1 t vanilla

Heat butter, sugar and lemon juice in saucepan until bubbly. Add peaches and cook 5 minutes or until peaches are heated through. Remove from heat and stir in vanilla. (*Great over ice cream, pound cake or pudding.*)

PEACH JAM

For something a little different try adding one tablespoon of rum to each jar before pouring the jam in.

3 lbs. peaches, peeled
2 T lemon juice
1 pkg. powered fruit pectin
5 1/2 c. sugar

Pit peaches and finely chop enough to make 1 qt. In a saucepan thoroughly mix peaches, lemon juice and pectin. Stir constantly over high heat until mixture boils. Add sugar, bring to a rolling boil and boil for 1 minute, stirring all the time. Remove jam into hot sterile jars and seal. Makes 6 to 7 cups.

PEACH CUSTARD PIE

1 unbaked 9-inch pie shell
1 c. sugar
3 eggs
2 T flour
2 T melted butter
1 T cream
4 c. sliced peaches

Beat together sugar, eggs, flour, butter and cream. Place peach slices on bottom of pie shell. Pour creamed mixture over peaches. Bake at 400 degrees for 10 minutes. Reduce heat to 375 degrees and continue baking another 40-45 minutes.

PEACH PECAN PIE

1/4 c. butter
1/4 c. brown sugar
3 T flour
2 t lemon juice
4 c. sliced peaches
1/2 c. pecans
1 unbaked pie shell

Cook butter, sugar and flour over medium heat until thickened. Add lemon juice. Mix in peaches and pour into pie shell. Sprinkle with pecans. Bake at 250 degrees 40 minutes.

PEACHES AND CREAM

4 peaches, peeled
1 c. sherry
1 T sugar
1 T red currant jelly
1 pt. vanilla ice cream

Cut peaches in half and pit. Heat sherry and sugar with pits and peach halves. Simmer for 30 minutes. Remove pits. Put peaches in serving dish and chill. Add jelly to wine mixture and cook until syrupy. Chill. Fill peach halves with ice cream and pour wine sauce over. Serves 4.

PEACH CORDIAL

3 lb. peaches
2 1/2 c. sugar
4 strips lemon peel
4 cinnamon sticks
6 whole cloves
1 qt. whiskey

In a gallon jar combine peaches, sugar, lemon peel and slices. Pour in whiskey and stir. Stir daily for one week. After two months strain mixture and bottle.

SPICED PEACHES

2 qt. small peaches
Whole cloves
2 1/2 c. brown sugar
1 c. cider vinegar
1 cinnamon stick, broken

Scald peaches and peel. Stick each with a clove. Bring sugar, vinegar and cinnamon to a boil. Add fruit and cook until tender, about 10 minutes. Pack in hot sterile jars, adding syrup to within 1/2-inch of top. Seal. Makes 4 pints.

PEACH SOUP

2 c. peaches, peeled
2 T lemon juice
2 T sugar
2 c. sweet white wine
1 small piece cinnamon stick
1/8 t almond extract

Pit peaches and puree in blender. Pour into bowl and cover with lemon juice and sugar. Bring wine and cinnamon stick to a boil and simmer 2 minutes. Strain and mix in extract. Mix into peaches and chill.

PEACH CRUMBLE

- 1/2 c. flour
- 1/2 c. rolled oats
- 1/2 c. brown sugar
- 1/4 t nutmeg
- 1/4 t salt
- 1/2 t cinnamon
- 1/8 t cloves
- 1/2 c. butter
- 4 c. peaches, sliced
- 1 t lemon juice
- 2 T water

Mix dry ingredients together. Stir in butter until mixture is crumbly. Put peaches in bottom of 8-inch square baking dish. Cover with lemon juice and water. Sprinkle crumb mixture over top and pat down. Bake at 350 degrees for 45 minutes.

Pears

PEARS HELENE

6-oz. pkg. chocolate chips
1/2 c. light corn syrup
1/4 c. evaporated milk
1 T butter
1/4 t vanilla
1 qt. vanilla ice cream
4 pears, peeled, cored, halved & cooked

In top of double boiler melt chocolate chips. Stir in corn syrup. Remove from heat and mix in milk, butter and vanilla. Cool. Spoon ice cream into 8 dessert dishes. Place a pear half in each dish. Spoon chocolate sauce on top. Serves 8.

PEAR SAUCE

4 pears, peeled, cored & quartered
1/2 c. sugar
1/2 c. water
Dash ginger
2 t lemon juice
1/2 t grated lemon rind
1/4 t vanilla

Cook pears in covered saucepan with sugar and water until tender, about 30 minutes. Mash with remaining ingredients. Serve warm over gingerbread or ice cream.

STUFFED PEAR SALAD

Peel, core and halve two pears. In a bowl, mix together equal parts of grated carrot and cheddar cheese. Stir in a small amount of French dressing. Stuff each pear half with mixture. Serve on a lettuce leaf for a lovely salad. Serves 4.

PEAR PIE

Pastry for 2-crust, 9-inch pie
5 pears, peeled, cored & sliced
3/4 c. brown sugar
Dash salt
1/4 t ginger
1/4 t mace
1 1/2 T cornstarch
3 T orange juice
1 t lemon juice
1 T butter

Place pear slices in pastry-lined pie shell. Combine dry ingredients and sprinkle over pears. Pour juices over mixture and dot with butter. Cover with top crust, slashing in center. Seal and bake at 425 degrees for 45-50 minutes.

BAKED PEARS

6 pears, unpeeled, halved & cored 1/2 c. water
1/2 c. brown sugar 1/4 t ginger
1/2 c. maple syrup

Place pears in baking dish. Combine remaining ingredients and pour over pears. Bake at 325 degrees for 1 hour. Add more water if needed to keep fruit from burning. Serves 6.

PEAR BREAD

1/2 c. butter
1 c. sugar
2 eggs
2 c. flour
1/2 t salt
1/2 t baking soda
1 t baking powder
1/8 t nutmeg
1/4 c. sour cream
1 c. coarsely chopped, cored pears
1 t vanilla

Cream butter and sugar. Beat in eggs one at a time. Combine dry ingredients; add to egg mixture. Mix in sour cream. Stir in pears and vanilla. Pour into buttered 9x5-inch loaf pan. Bake at 350 degrees for 1 hour.

Plums

PLUM KUCHEN

1 1/2 c. flour
4 T sugar
2 t baking powder
1/2 t salt
3 T butter
1 egg
6 T milk
5 plums, halved
1/2 c. brown sugar
1 t cinnamon
1/4 c. flour
1/4 c. soft butter

Cut butter into flour, sugar, baking powder and salt. In a separate bowl, mix egg and milk together. Pour into dry ingredients and stir. Spread in buttered 8-inch square baking dish. Place plum halves on top (cut side up). Combine brown sugar, cinnamon, flour and butter. Sprinkle over plums. Bake at 450 degrees 25-30 minutes.

PLUM MUFFINS

3/4 lb. plums, chopped
2 1/2 c. flour
2 t baking soda
1/2 t salt
1 c. sugar
1/4 c. melted butter
2 eggs, slightly beaten
1/2 c. milk
1/2 c. chopped walnuts
1 T sugar

Sprinkle plums with 1 T flour and toss lightly. In a large bowl, combine flour, baking soda and salt with 1 c. sugar. In another bowl, stir butter, eggs and milk until smooth. Add liquid ingredients to dry ones, stirring just until moistened. Fold in plums and walnuts. Spoon batter into muffin cups, filling 2/3 full. Sprinkle 1 T sugar on top of batter. Bake at 400 degrees 20-25 minutes. Makes 18.

SPICED PLUMS

3 lb. plums
1 lb. sugar
8 whole cloves
2 cinnamon sticks, broken
1 c. cider vinegar

Prick each plum in several places with a needle. Place in a large pan. In a separate saucepan, combine ingredients and bring to a boil. Pour boiling liquid over plums. Let stand 20 minutes. Drain liquid back into saucepan and boil again. Pour over plums and let stand again for 20 minutes. Drain and boil liquid once more. Add plums and let boil 5 minutes. Ladle into hot sterile jars. Let stand 4 weeks before using. Makes 2 1/2 pints.

Raspberries

PATRIOT'S PIE

10-inch graham cracker crust
1 pt. whipping cream
3 T powdered sugar
1 t almond extract
1 pt. raspberries
1 c. blueberries

Whip cream until thick. Add powdered sugar and extract, blending well. Spread on pie shell. Arrange raspberries around edge and mound blueberries in center.

RASPBERRY DESSERT

- 1 3-oz. pkg. raspberry flavored gelatin
- 1/2 c. sugar
- 1 c. hot water
- 1 c. raspberries
- 1 c. applesauce
- 2 c. miniature marshmallows
- 1 c. sour cream

Dissolve gelatin and sugar in hot water. Stir in raspberries and applesauce. Chill until firm. Mix together marshmallows and sour cream. Spread on top. Serves 4.

RASPBERRY COBBLER

4 c. raspberries
2/3 c. sugar
1/2 t lemon juice
2 T butter
1 1/2 c. biscuit mix
3 T melted butter
1 egg, slightly beaten
1/2 c. milk
Whipped cream or ice cream

Toss berries with sugar and lemon juice. Place in buttered 10x6-inch baking dish. Dot with 2 T butter. Combine biscuit mix, melted butter, egg and milk. With a spoon, drop dough over fruit. Bake 30-35 minutes. Serve warm with whipped cream or ice cream. Serves 6.

RASPBERRY PIE

9 inch baked pie shell
6 c. raspberries
1/2 c. water
2/3 c. sugar
3 T cornstarch
1/2 pt. whipped cream
2 T powdered sugar

Mash berries and strain seeds out through a sieve. Place berries, water, sugar and cornstarch in a saucepan and cook, stirring constantly until thick. Cool and pour into a pie shell. Chill until set. Whip cream. Stir in sugar and spread on top of pie before serving.

RASPBERRY JAM

3 c. raspberries
3 c. sugar
1/4 bottle liquid fruit pectin

Crush berries and mix with sugar. Let stand 20 minutes. Stir in pectin and fill hot sterile jars with jam. Seal. Let stand at room temperature overnight. Store in refrigerator or freezer. Makes about 4 8-oz. jars.

RASPBERRY SAUCE

1 pt. raspberries
1/4 c. water
1/4 c. sugar
1 T cornstarch
1/2 t lemon juice

Mash berries and strain out seeds through a sieve. Put berries in saucepan with remaining ingredients. Cook over medium heat until thick, stirring constantly. Makes about 1 cup. *(Great on ice cream, vanilla pudding or pound cake. You can also make Peach Melba with this sauce by pouring it over ice cream and peaches.)*

Rhubarb

RHUBARB CREAM PIE

9-inch pie shell with lattice top	Pinch salt
1 1/2 c. sugar	3 eggs
1/4 c. flour	4 c. rhubarb
3/4 t nutmeg	2 T butter

Mix sugar, flour, nutmeg and salt. Beat with eggs. Cut rhubarb into 1-inch pieces and mix in. Pour filling into shell; top with lattice crust. Bake at 400 degrees 50-60 minutes. *(If you use rhubarb in only one recipe, it should be this one. Fantastic!)*

RHUBARB CREAM CAKE

1 c. cream	1 1/2 t baking powder
1 egg	1 c. rhubarb, cut into 2-inch pieces
3/4 c. sugar	
1 1/4 c. flour	1/4 c. sugar
1/8 t. nutmeg	1 t cinnamon

Beat cream, egg and sugar. Add flour, baking powder and nutmeg. Pour into a buttered 8-inch square cake pan. Spread rhubarb over cake. Bake 40 minutes at 375 degrees. Sprinkle sugar and cinnamon on top. Return to oven for 5 more minutes. Serve with cream.

BAKED RHUBARB

4 c. rhubarb
1 1/2 c. sugar
1/4 t cinnamon
1/8 t nutmeg
1/8 t cloves
Juice and rind of one orange

Cut rhubarb into 2-inch pieces. Mix with remaining ingredients. Cover and bake at 350 degrees for 45-50 minutes. Serve as is or with ice cream.

RHUBARB-STRAWBERRY JAM

5 c. rhubarb, diced
4 c. sugar
1 3-oz. box strawberry gelatin

Let rhubarb and sugar stand overnight, stirring often. In the morning, boil 10 minutes. Add gelatin and mix well. Pour into jars and store in refrigerator or freezer. Makes about 6 8-oz. jars.

RHUBARB BREAD

2 1/2 c. flour
1 t salt
1 t baking soda
1 1/4 c. brown sugar
1 egg, beaten
1/2 t vanilla
2/3 c. salad oil
1 c. sour milk
2 c. rhubarb, diced
1/2 c. chopped walnuts

Sift together flour, salt, soda and sugar. Beat egg, vanilla and salad oil. Stir in milk. Blend into sifted ingredients. Stir in rhubarb and walnuts. Pour into 2 buttered loaf pans. Sprinkle with topping. Bake at 325 degrees for 60 minutes.

TOPPING
1/2 c. brown sugar
1 T. butter

RHUBARB UPSIDE DOWN CAKE

2 T butter	2 c. flour
1 c. brown sugar	3 t baking powder
2 c. rhubarb, cut in 1-inch pieces	1/4 t salt
1/2 c. butter	1/4 t nutmeg
1 c. sugar	1 t vanilla
2 eggs	3/4 c. milk

Melt 2 T butter in bottom of square baking dish and stir in brown sugar and rhubarb. In a separate bowl, beat butter and sugar. Add eggs and beat well. Sift together flour, baking powder, salt and nutmeg. Add alternately to batter with vanilla and milk. Pour over rhubarb and bake at 375 degrees for 45 minutes.

RHUBARB TORTE

1 c. flour
6 T powdered sugar
1/2 c. soft butter
1 1/2 c. sugar
1/4 c. flour
3/4 t baking powder
1/2 t. cinnamon
1/4 t salt
2 c. rhubarb, finely chopped
1/4 c. walnuts
2 eggs, well beaten
1 t vanilla extract

Mix flour, powdered sugar and butter together. Pat into buttered 8x11-inch baking pan. Bake at 350 degrees for 15 minutes. Combine remaining ingredients, mixing well. Spread over baked crust and bake at 350 degrees 45 minutes. Chill. Serve with whipped cream.

RHUBARB CUSTARD

6 c. rhubarb
2 c. sugar
1 T butter
5 T flour
2 t nutmeg
2 eggs, beaten

Cut rhubarb into 1-inch pieces and place in greased square baking dish. Mix remaining ingredients together and spoon over rhubarb. Bake at 400 degrees for 20 minutes. Reduce heat to 350 degrees and bake for 20 more minutes. Serves 4-6.

Strawberries

STRAWBERRY SHORTCAKE

1 qt. strawberries	2 T sugar
1 c. sugar	1/3 c. shortening
2 c. flour	3/4 c. milk
2 t baking powder	Butter
1 t salt	Whipped cream

Slice strawberries, reserving a few whole ones for garnish. Mix with sugar and set aside. Sift dry ingredients and cut in shortening; blend until mixture is crumbly. Make a well and pour in milk. Stir and form dough into a ball. Place on lightly floured board and knead about 15 times. Pat out dough to 1/2-inch thickness. Cut into rounds with a 3-inch cutter. Spread half the rounds with soft butter. Top with remaining rounds. Place on baking sheet and bake at 450 degrees for 10-15 minutes. Split shortcakes and spoon half the strawberries over bottom layer. Top with shortcakes and more strawberries. Add a spoonful of whipped cream on top. Garnish with a few whole strawberries. Makes 6.

STRAWBERRY-FILLED PANCAKES

1 1/4 c. flour
1 1/2 c. milk
5 eggs
1/4 c. melted butter
1/2 t salt
3 T sugar
3 c. sliced strawberries
1/2 c. sugar
Powdered sugar

Make a batter from the flour, milk, eggs, butter, salt and 3 T sugar. In a separate bowl mix together strawberries and 1/2 c. sugar. In a large skillet, melt 1 T butter for each pancake. Add 1/6 of the batter and cook until golden brown before turning to brown other side. Keep pancakes warm. Place 1/2 c. strawberries on edge of each pancake and roll up. Sprinkle with powdered sugar. Serve with whipped or sour cream. Makes 6.

STRAWBERRY JAM

4 c. strawberries
7 c. sugar
1 T lemon juice

Slice strawberries and combine with other ingredients. Let stand overnight. Bring to a boil, stirring often. Cook until syrup is thick. Skim off foam. Ladle into hot sterile jars and seal. Makes about 4 8-oz. jars.

STRAWBERRY PUNCH

2 c. strawberries, mashed
1 1/2 c. lemon juice
1 1/2 c. orange juice
1 1/4 c. sugar
1 c. water
6 c. weak tea

Mix berries and juices. Boil sugar and water to make a syrup; add to berries with tea. Pour into punch bowl. Garnish with strawberry halves. Makes 2 1/2 quarts.

STRAWBERRY BREAD

1/2 c. butter
1 c. sugar
1/2 t almond extract
2 eggs, separated
2 c. flour
1 t baking powder
1 t baking soda
1 t salt
1 c. strawberries, crushed
1 T sugar

Cream butter, sugar and almond extract. Beat in egg yolks. Sift flour, baking powder, soda and salt. Mix into creamed mixture alternately with strawberries. Beat egg whites until stiff. Fold into batter. Pour into a buttered loaf pan. Sprinkle sugar on top. Bake at 325 degrees for 50-60 minutes.

STRAWBERRY TOPPING

    1 c. strawberries, sliced
    Dash salt
    1 egg white
    1 c. powdered sugar
    1 t vanilla

Beat strawberries, salt, egg white and powdered sugar until stiff. Beat in vanilla until very stiff. Serve on angel cake or fruit.

STRAWBEERY MOLDED CREAM
1 pkg. unflavored gelatin
3/4 c. sugar
1 c. cream
1/2 pt. sour cream
2 c. strawberries, sliced
1/2 c. sugar

Stir the sugar and gelatin in double boiler. Add cream and stir over hot water until gelatin and sugar dissolves. Chill until mixture begins to set. Fold in sour cream. Turn into mold and chill until set. Unmold and serve with strawberries mixed with sugar. Serves 6.

GLAZED STRAWBERRY PIE

Baked 9" pie shell
1 qt. strawberries
1 3-oz. pkg. cream cheese, softened
1 1/2 c. strawberry juice
3 T cornstarch

Spread cream cheese on bottom of pastry shell. Cover with half the berries. Mash and strain rest of berries until juice is extracted. Bring juice to a boil. Boil 1 minute. Pour over berries in pie shell. Chill 2 hours. Serve with whip cream.

STRAWBERRY-TOMATO PIE

10-inch unbaked pie shell
  with lattice top
1 qt. strawberries
1 c. sugar
4 tomatoes, peeled and cubed
6 T flour
1/4 t cinnamon
3 T sugar
3 T butter

Mix strawberries and sugar. Let stand until juice is drawn out, about 1 hour. Pour half the strawberries and juice into pie shell. Sprinkle with half the flour and cinnamon. Top with half the tomatoes and half the sugar. Dot with half the butter. Repeat layers. Cover with lattice top. Bake at 450 degrees for 15 minutes. Lower heat to 400 degrees and bake 25 more minutes. Chill and serve with whipped cream.

STRAWBERRY SYRUP

1 T cornstarch
1/3 c. water
1/4 c. sugar
2 c. sliced strawberries
1 t lemon juice

In a small saucepan, mix cornstarch and water. Add sugar and bring to a boil, stirring constantly, until mixture is clear and thick. Add strawberries and lemon juice. Heat through. *(A nice topping for pancakes or waffles.)*

STRAWBERRY CAKE

1 c. flour
1/2 c. sugar
2 t baking powder
Dash of salt
1 egg
2 T melted butter
1/2 c. milk
1 1/2 c. sliced strawberries

Sift dry ingredients. Add egg, butter and milk; beat for 2 minutes. Pour into buttered 8-inch square pan. Top with strawberries.

Sprinkle with topping of:
1/2 c. flour
1/2 c. sugar
1/4 c. butter
1/4 c. chopped walnuts

Bake in a 375 degree oven for 35 minutes.

CHILLED STRAWBERRY SOUP

- 1 qt. strawberries
- 1/2 c. water
- 1/2 c. orange juice
- 1/2 c. sugar
- 2 c. yogurt

Mix all ingredients in blender. Chill. Serves 6.

Watermelon

PICKLED WATERMELON RIND

7 c. watermelon rind
3 T salt
1 qt. cold water
1 qt. boiling water
1 pt. cider vinegar
6 c. sugar
1 1/2 t cinnamon
1 1/2 t cloves
1/4 t nutmeg

Cut rind into small pieces, paring away the green and pink. Use 7 cups of rind and cover with quart of cold water with salt mixed in. Cover and let stand overnight. Drain. Cover with fresh water and cook 8-10 minutes. Drain again. Mix together quart boiling water, vinegar, sugar and ground spices and boil again, stirring until sugar dissolves. Boil 5 minutes. Add drained rind. Boil gently until rind is transparent, about 40-45 minutes. Ladle into hot, sterile jars and seal. Let stand about 4 weeks before using. Makes about 2 pints.

MELON DESSERT

Place equal parts of watermelon, cantaloupe and honeydew balls in separate glass serving dishes. Top each with a teaspoon of frozen lemonade concentrate.

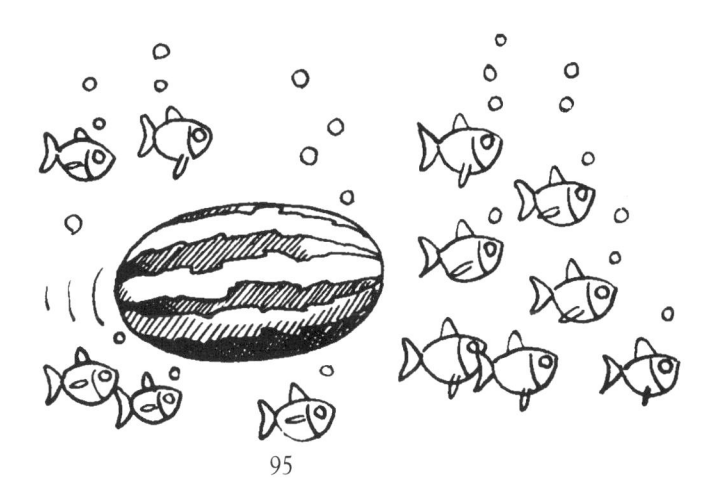

For a brochure describing other **eberly press** books, please write to:

eberly press
1004 Michigan Ave.
East Lansing, MI 48823